# ANOTHER FACE OF GOD

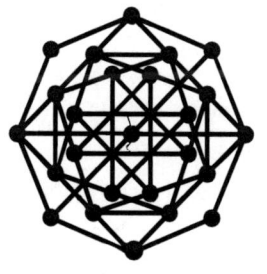

Joseph, the Dreamer

# ANOTHER FACE OF GOD

by Giuseppe Giucastro
(with Judith P. Foard-Giucastro)

SMALL BATCH BOOKS

AMHERST, MASSACHUSETTS

Copyright © 2017 by Giuseppe Giucastro

All rights reserved.
No part of this book may be copied,
transmitted, or reproduced without permission.
Printed in the United States of America
on SFI™-certified, acid-free paper.

Designed by Lisa Vega
Author photo by Judith P. Foard-Giucastro

ISBN: 978-0-9829758-6-2
Library of Congress Control Number 2017942224

493 SOUTH PLEASANT STREET
AMHERST, MASSACHUSETTS 01002
413.230.3943
SMALLBATCHBOOKS.COM

*The True Ten Commandments of God*

In truth, I imagine that this was what God wanted to say about the Ten Commandments:

"If you follow and obey my commands, you'll have a better life on Earth.

If you choose to do evil, you will be punished by your laws, but not by me. You are free to choose."

# CONTENTS

*Foreword*

Chapter One
*New York City, 1977*

Chapter Two
*Conversation with the Holy Spirit #1*

Chapter Three
*Conversation with the Holy Spirit #2*

Chapter Four
*Conversation with the Holy Spirit #3*

Chapter Five
*Conversation with My Granddaughter:
A Vision of the Afterlife*

*Acknowledgments*

# FOREWORD

Buongiorno. My name is Giuseppe, or Joseph in English. I was born in 1940 in a small mountain town in Sicily called Buccheri, about sixty miles from the ocean. When I left Sicily at the age of eighteen, I moved to Venezuela, and then later to the United States, living in New York City; Hartford, Connecticut; Springfield and later Westfield, Massachusetts. I have been a hairdresser and salon owner, a restaurant cook and pizzeria owner, and now I am a writer. I have been married three times (the third time is the charm?). And a long, long time ago, I had an amazing dream that greatly changed my life. It was because of the dream that I began to write, and I would like to share some of these writings with you.

\* \* \* \*

Forty years ago, I dreamt that a group of influential and famous people—Albert Einstein, Sigmund Freud, Pope John XXIII, Orson Welles, Khalil Gibran, Nostradamus, and Michelangelo—asked me to be their intermediary to complete two missions. One mission would be for the benefit of the planet Earth, and the other would be for the afterlife.

These seven wise people began to impart a new awareness of many subjects in my mind: Albert Einstein on the theory of the quantum computer; Sigmund Freud on the perceptions of dreams; Orson Welles on how to become an actor and a director in life; Pope John XXIII, the Spiritual Father, on the concept of another face of God; Kahlil Gibran on knowing thyself; Nostradamus on the ability to see into the future; and Michelangelo on the design of a visually animated world for all the souls inside the sea.

In the beginning, it was very difficult to accept this new awareness that my mind now held. Along the way, and in many subsequent dreams, I had lots of conversations with each one of these seven people, and each taught me something very special. Over all these years, with my mind bombarded with so many new ideas, I came to have a new awareness of myself. I wondered why I was chosen to be the intermediary for these seven wise persons and what kind of mission it was that they had for me. I knew that these were only dreams—but they seemed so real to me. I thought that perhaps if I started to tell my story from the beginning, by the end I would be able to put the pieces of this dream-puzzle together.

I hope I have found the proper words to share my fascinating dreams with you. I hope that some scientists will take note of what I have written about this mission for the afterlife.

I know that much of my story is based in imagination... but imagination can become reality. So let's make believe that Joseph's dreams *are* real.

CHAPTER 1

*New York City, 1977*

One night, when I was thirty-seven years old, I dreamt of being beyond space. I saw a bright light in front of a big box and heard a woman's voice as if coming from a computer, saying, "We are a commission of Spiritual Souls from an invisible planet called Iyakacquasia." (I instinctively knew the spelling of this word.) "Known only by the Holy Spirit and the Spiritual Commission, Iyakacquasia is an invisible planet, a depository of human souls, energy, and knowledge. The good and imaginative are the fundamental basis of our existence." It continued: "We have prepared a mission for you. You have been chosen to organize our vision on Earth and in the afterlife. Inside this chest, you will find everything you need to learn about and understand your mission and what your plans will be. You will have until the end of the year 1999 for acquiring the knowledge of our vision and of our existence.

"We know how to communicate with you, and we are always with you to help you as best we can. One day, with the help of technology, we hope that you will figure out a way to communicate with us. Good luck."

Those were the last words I heard. I tried to say something but could not. Then on a big screen, I saw images of the seven wise people from the past. I saw the face of Albert Einstein with a phrase that said, "Imagination is more important than knowledge." I also saw the faces of Michelangelo, Orson Welles, Kahlil Gibran, Pope John XXIII, Nostradamus, and Sigmund Freud.

Then it all disappeared, except for the large chest that was in front of me. I knew that I was dreaming, and I somehow realized that everything would soon disappear. I opened the chest, and inside I found it full of books of knowledge. I quickly flipped through all the books and was amazed at how many words and phrases I understood that I had never used before. I also saw a bag with a sign that said, "A bag full of dreams and projects," as well as a Bible and a cross that had several words written on it.

I remember saying to myself, "How can I understand all those fancy words written in English?" I only went to school through the elementary level, and English was not my first language. Then I wondered, "They, whoever they are—why did they choose me?" Later on in the dream, I saw myself lying on a bed surrounded by people dressed in white coats ready to operate on the inside of my head, near my left ear. Instead of tools, they were going to use their fingers, from which rays were emanating. The room was like being inside a cave, and the walls gave off thin strips of color, as if there were drops of water falling from them. Outside, I saw a beach—a sea that was so calm, it looked like blue velvet—and a clear sky with a big rainbow of beautiful colors. Then, suddenly, I woke up in my apartment in New York City.

I was fascinated with the dream. It seemed so real. I went to the bathroom and looked in the mirror, and for the first time ever, I really looked in my eyes, and as I did, I felt as if I were seeing inside myself. For many years, working as a hairdresser, there was always a mirror in front of me, but I don't remember ever watching my eyes while I worked. I was focused on the head of the client.

That next morning, while eating breakfast, I took out a notebook and started writing down some of the words I had seen in the dream, words from the books of knowledge in the chest, words I had not known but now I wanted to understand. I also made a drawing of the cross I saw and began filling it with the words that were on it. Then I left my apartment.

I walked down Broadway, not knowing specifically where I was going. When I stopped in front of a bookstore, an inner force seemed to be pushing me inside. Not

> **EVIL**
>
> LA CROCE DI VENT'ANNI FÀ?
> LA CROCE DI OGGI –
> Why?
>
> | JESUS (LOVE) | GOD – (LIFE) | SATAN (EVIL) |
> |---|---|---|
> | | CONTROL | |
> | | IMMAGINATION | |
> | | KNOWLEDGE | |
> | | FAMILY | |
> | | HOME | |
> | | RESPONSABILITY | |
> | | WORKING | |
> | | MOTIVATION | |
> | | SECURITY | |
> | | FOUNDATION | |
> | | SUCCESS | |
> | | SPIRITUAL | |
> | | CARE | |
> | | SHARE | |
> | | RESPECT | |
> | | MONEY | |
> | | PLEASURE | |
> | | REALITY | |
> | | BIBLE | |
> | | PHYLOSOPHY | |
> | | HOPE | |
> | | SIMPLICITY | |

knowing what I was looking for, I began to read titles on books and headlines on papers. When I saw something with words that resembled those in my dream, I put it aside. When I saw a Bible, I was surprised that it had the same cover of the Bible I had seen in my dream. In the end, I bought the Bible, a Webster's dictionary, and some books and magazines. When I returned to my apartment, I began to read and write with the help of the English dictionary. I started to analyze the English words I saw, trying to better understand their meaning.

From that day on, my inner life changed completely. I felt as if I had acquired a new insight. I was infused with a desire to learn more about why I had been chosen. My dream seemed so very real to me. I remembered all details of it, but I was especially taken by the phrase of Albert Einstein—"imagination is more important than knowledge"—and the voice of the woman who told me that I had been chosen to complete a mission. But what kind of mission was I to accomplish?

I spent every night for many years reading, writing, and analyzing the words I needed to understand with the help of the dictionary.

With the beginning of the year 2000, I knew that my time to learn had expired. Now everything depended on me. Years ago, my old friend and private professor, Joe Tobia, from Westfield, Massachusetts, told me that my vision and my intents were beautiful but too difficult to understand. He said, "Only you can find a way to make them clear. I will write these words for you:

IF IT IS TO BE ... IT IS UP TO ME.

When you understand the meaning of this phrase, then you will be ready to fulfill your mission."

CHAPTER 2

*Conversation with the Holy Spirit #1*

One night I dreamt that energy in the form of an angel appeared to me. The angel was dressed in a strange outfit, not the usual flowing white gown with wings. On her back was some sort of electronic machine and in her hand was a small, pistol-like instrument that began to shoot energy into my whole body and mind. This went on for a few minutes, and then I saw the tree of knowledge and a phrase that said, "Now you are ready to start with God's new plan for the afterlife." Then the angel disappeared.

Okay, I thought. What could this mean? First, I imagined that the Holy Spirit is a woman, and about fifty years before, Jesus had turned to the Holy Spirit, who was standing to the left of God, and said, "Sis, now it is your turn to do something different for humanity."

"What do you have in mind?" asked the Holy Spirit.

"Well, as you know, from the beginning of time, God has always challenged humans to develop the resources on Earth. God did not make things for them but instead expected them to discover the raw materials He had put on Earth for their use in creating a better life. Think of the discovery of fire or the invention of the wheel, for example," responded Jesus.

"Or how iron ore was used to make steel," added the Holy Spirit. "Nowadays, humans have even developed technology to the point that instant communication is possible all over the world. But how does this tie in with what you have planned for me?"

"I am asking you now to accept the challenge that God wants to give humanity, to create a new world for the afterlife using the tools of technology."

"What? What are you asking me to do?" asked the Holy Spirit. "How can I help create a new world for the afterlife when all the souls are in a semiconscious state on the invisible planet of Iyakacquasia awaiting your return to Earth?"

"God has decided that these souls need a more colorful world to live in right now. You know that at present they are only awakened when there is thunder and lightning."

"Well, how am I to do that? The job seems impossible!"

"This is the plan: You are to make contact with seven wise souls of your choosing who are at rest on this invisible planet. Wake them up and explain to them the details of this mission. They, in their wisdom, will be able to develop the plan for bringing animation to the afterlife using technological resources from the Earth."

"But how can they direct a mission like this when they live on an invisible planet?"

"The seven souls will search the world for a simple Earthling who has little education but much wisdom and common sense. Once they have chosen someone, they will communicate with that person through dreams. In turn, this person will have the mission of finding scientists who, with their technological knowledge and creativity, will be able to develop this new colorful world of the afterlife."

The conversation ended, and the Holy Spirit immediately went to the invisible planet of the afterlife. After much contemplation, she chose seven wise souls once well known on Earth for their genius. The Holy Spirit then awakened Albert Einstein, Pope John XXIII, Sigmund Freud, Orson Welles, Kahlil Gibran, Nostradamus, and Michelangelo for this important mission. After a worldwide search, these seven souls, now known as the Spiritual Commission of the Souls, selected a man named Joseph to help them with the mission, and they began to share their wisdom with him through dreams.

Well, as you know, I am that Joseph. And over many years of many dreams, I have had many dialogues, not only with the seven wise souls, but also with the Holy

Spirit. It was She who told me that I had been chosen to help Her with God's new plan for the afterlife. After receiving many messages from the voice of the Holy Spirit about this new plan of God's, I began to ask questions and demand some answers.

"You say that you are the Holy Spirit. Why can I not see you? I only hear a woman's voice."

"For now, you only hear my voice. With time, you will see me."

"Okay," I said, "let's assume that this experience is real, and let's say that I will be doing what you are asking me to do. Can I have the freedom to ask you any questions and make any comments?"

The Holy Spirit replied, "I like it when questions are asked. You will have the freedom to ask me anything."

"Will you answer me with simple words?"

"I promise I will."

"Correct me if I am wrong, but first, I need to understand what my role will be in this new plan of God's for the afterlife. Holy Spirit, can I call you Boss?"

"Yes, you can! I kind of like that."

(I was thinking that this vision with the voice of the Holy Spirit could be the key to this new awareness.)

After a few moments, I called out, "Boss, are you still here?"

"I am always here," she responded.

"While you are here, are you going to preach and perform miracles like Jesus did?"

"No, my mission is not about prayers, preaching, or miracles. That was Jesus' mission. My mission is about the formulation of a new world for the souls. Also, I am here to help fix things on Earth."

"Boss, things here on Earth are really bad. We have a number of powerful people in government who still believe in wars and don't care how many innocent people get killed. We need to find a way to stop all this nonsense."

"Well, Joseph, that's why you were chosen. This is where your challenge begins. Good luck, and always remember, *if it is to be, it is up to me!* (And by that I mean you.)"

Before continuing with this imaginary journey toward finding a new truth about another face of God, and learning how to create for Him this new world for the afterlife, it is proper to make some assumptions. Joseph's visions, my visions, have nothing to do with traditional religion, and it is important that we keep an open mind. Although in the past I was not active in church life, I have always had a strong belief in God, in Jesus Christ, and in the Holy Spirit. I also believe that the Bible is the basis of God's plan.

I truly believe that God challenges us humans to

improve upon His creation and also to learn more about the afterlife. He challenges those of us on Earth to go beyond prayer and to work to discover what he has placed here for our use—and to develop those resources for the use of mankind. I believe in a God who is revealed in the harmony of His creation, not only a God who cares for the fate and actions of human beings.

CHAPTER 3

*Conversation with the Holy Spirit #2*

"Hey, Boss. Can we talk?"

"Sure. What's on your mind?"

"I don't know, Boss. I just want to talk."

"I am listening."

"Boss, I am trying to understand what's happening to me. Who am I, really?"

"That is up to you. You know who you are and why you were chosen, and you have to accept it. I can't help you with that."

"You are right, Boss. I know that you know that *I know* who I am, and I know that you know that... I guess I am a little scared."

"I don't blame you, for I would be scared, too, if I were in your shoes."

"Thanks, Boss. That makes me feel better that you understand, but can you imagine the public reaction when I claim that I, Joseph, was chosen by the Holy Spirit to help with God's new plan for the afterlife? They will think I'm crazy."

"I am sure they will. Just be yourself, and everything will be okay. Trust me."

"I do trust you. I just want you to trust me, too. I know what I must do, and to do so, I need to talk with you like we are two best friends who share their lives and their thoughts. Can we do that?"

"Of course. I'd like that."

"Boss, today I had a very bad day. I don't like it when I lose control. Every time I feel very sure of what I should do, a big *BOOM* hits me as if the devil is inside of me, confusing my mind. This has happened to me too many times. Boss, is the devil real?"

"Of course the devil is real. He is also part of God's creation."

"Boss, that's very confusing. It is not easy to understand how we humans should behave. On the one hand, Jesus said that if we follow Him, we will have a good life on Earth and then will have eternal life with Him. On the other hand, Satan said that if we follow him, we will get all kinds of goodies like money, sex, power, fame, and so on. Boss, with all due respect, if that is the truth, I don't think that's fair."

"Not fair? I don't agree with you. Like I said before, Satan was also in God's plan. Tell me, Joe—you don't mind if I call you Joe?"

"I like that, Boss! As you were saying?"

"On the other side, God also gives humans the freedom to choose and to make their own decisions. Do you get my point?"

"I do, Boss. I've always believed that there should be nothing wrong with having lots of money and living the high life. Why can't we have both?"

"Bingo! You hit it right on the nose."

"I have a silly question, Boss. What do you guys do for fun?"

"What do you mean by that? Nobody has asked us that question before. Good question, Joseph."

"You see, Boss, I have read many different Bibles and never have read anything about what God, you, and Jesus do for fun."

"You are making a very good point. I see that you really understand God's new challenge. Even though I know the answer, I can't tell you. Not yet."

"Why not, Boss?"

"Remember that even we have rules that we must respect, because that is part of God's plan. What I can say is that you are making a very important observation."

"Boss, today at Bible study, I realized that some of the people there could be part of this story. What do you think?"

"I saw that, too. In your group there seem to be some

very devout people with many talents. Talk to them and start to make offers that they can't refuse."

"Boss, that was the mafia's motto."

"So . . . why not? It worked for them."

"Yes, it sure worked for the mafia. Boss, I like the way you talk and see things. You seem to be completely different from Jesus. That's neat—as my granddaughter would say."

"Are you saying that you don't like the way Jesus spoke?"

"Of course not, Boss. Jesus' philosophy and teachings were just different from yours. My relationship with Jesus has always been very good, but some of the words and many of the descriptions in both the Old and New Testaments about God, Jesus, and you seem very contradictory to me. I am sure other people feel that way, too."

"That's another job for you—to find a way to help resolve those contradictions that you humans often accumulate in your minds. I saw after Jesus left the Earth what all the churches have done to honor us. It is both good and bad."

"That's a big job, Boss. Where do I start?"

"You have started already. Keep asking me the right questions, and I will lead the way."

"Back to reality. . . . Holy shit!!!!!"

"Joe, I take that as a compliment."

"You bet, Boss! I came to a conclusion that from now on, no more excuses about protecting anyone's feelings toward me. I hope I don't need to give up my family and money to follow you, like Jesus asked his disciples to do."

"I will never ask you to do that—and neither was that Jesus' intention. He was asking them to leave all possessions behind temporarily, family included, but not to abandon them. On the contrary, Jesus meant to say, 'Follow me until you have learned more about my message. Then go back to your home and family and start to spread the word of the Son of God.'"

"I know that, Boss, but when I read the Bible, many parts seem confusing."

"That's why humans have been given the freedom to interpret what fits for them."

"That makes a lot of sense. Boss, while we are on the subject of the Bible, I remember in one of my dreams you asked me to write a new message in your name, and I asked you where I should start. I asked you if I should use the Bible as a mentor. You said that was good idea."

"Yes! I remember saying that. Why do you mention that now?"

"I don't know. But when the time comes for me to stand up and say aloud, 'I am now ready,' I promise you I will do whatever needs to be done to help you with God's new plan. And, Boss, perhaps now I should start to listen more than talk."

"I agree with you. But you don't need to show others a new way or a new writing to convince them that you are capable."

"I understand why you would say that, Boss. My mind continues to torture me. It is as if an invisible force keeps putting negative thoughts in my head. When that happens, I get new ideas, and I begin to get new visions of how I should convince others of my accomplishments. Am I going crazy, Boss?"

"You know that you are not. You may have all the reasons in the world to wonder if all this is for real. I suggest you continue to think, for now, that all is both a fruit of your imagination, and in some ways also reality. Go back to what you once wrote: 'imagination vs. reality.'"

"I just finished reading those words in my mind, imagination vs. reality. That's it, Boss. It says everything. Thanks for illuminating my mind. Yes! I am ready now."

"Good work, Joseph! We have lots left to do. Let this journey continue. I promise you that I will always be nearby."

"Thanks, Boss!"

"By the way, Joe, I have a question for you. Why do you think of me, the Holy Spirit, as a woman?"

"Well, first of all, when I hear you, I hear the voice of

a woman. Also, in the Old Testament, we humans often see God as a macho type who punishes those who do not obey Him. In the New Testament we see his Son, Jesus, as one who has the attributes of a milder form of man and who teaches love and forgiveness. In the Holy Spirit, I see the attributes of a woman who emphasizes peace and tenderness. Today, I believe that the Holy Spirit is a woman who helps us carry on with God's plans for the afterlife. I believe that for us humans the Father, Son, and Holy Spirit should be seen in both their masculine and feminine roles. Seeing the Holy Spirit as a woman can show the world those qualities of the Divine—such as peacefulness and compassion—that we often associate with womanhood.

"We human beings sooner or later ask the following questions: Who are we? Where do we come from? Where are we headed? When we ask these questions, we begin to take more seriously our inner life, the place where we are more able to commune with God.

"In the Old Testament, God, our Father, after creating the world, used Moses to proclaim to His chosen people the Ten Commandments, which were to serve as a fundamental basis for a just human society. In the New Testament, He used an angel who spoke to Mary, a lowly maiden, in her dreams and gave her the message that she would give birth to a son, Jesus, who is the Son of God. In the New Testament, we see another face of God. Through His Son, He shows such compassion and is willing to have His Son die for us. Jesus also shows us through example and teaching how to live peacefully and obtain eternal life.

"The Holy Spirit is the one who, through our souls, guides us in this life; but Satan, or evil, if you prefer to call it, also comes into the picture. Within us, there is often a battle between the good that Jesus instills in us and the bad that evil tempts us with. In these struggles, I often wonder if we humans are robots that do not have total free will. Are we controlled either by God through the Holy Spirit or by the power of Satan or evil? The good news, though, is that we are made in the image of God and are in some mysterious fashion programmed to transform His creation, for better or for worse. Without any doubt, God's intelligence is incomparable and superior to ours, but it is also true that He needs us to discover the resources that He has put in His creation and that He expects us to develop. And now, Boss, I realize again that maybe I need to talk less and listen more."

CHAPTER 4

*Conversation with the Holy Spirit #3*

"Boss, for me to do my job well, I need to understand what God's purpose is for humans. For example, why did God put the tree of knowledge and tree of life in the center of the garden if he knew that Adam and Eve would disobey him? It does not make any sense at all."

"Excellent question, Joe—a question that theologians, philosophers, and believers have been puzzling over for hundreds, if not thousands, of years. I will try to give you some guidance the best way I can. Remember that all that was created is a part of God's plan."

"Yeah, you keep saying that, but I need more support from you, especially when the time comes for me to go public with God's new plan for the afterlife. For it to be accepted, I need to be very convincing—you know what I mean?"

"Of course I do. But I need to be very careful with my answer. You are asking me some very direct and important questions—you know what *I* mean. To the question of the tree of knowledge, Joe, you're in the right direction. Start to use the words *assume* and *if*. Then let imagination do the rest."

"Okay, Boss. I understand you. Perhaps now is the time for me to start using the Bible as a guide—it's the only source of information I have about you guys, and there is much I need to understand. So whatever I will ask you about this dream of mine, I will try to be very humble. Let's begin with some questions I have.

"Boss, in one of my dreams, I saw seventy envelopes, and in Genesis, I read something about seventy people being promised a future of greatness by God. Could seventy be the number of disciples I need to have for fulfilling God's new plan?"

"That's a good observation, but it's not important at the moment."

"Okay, Boss, my next questions are why did God create humans in His own image, and what was His main purpose for creating humans?"

"One question at a time, Joseph. Why did we create humans in our own image? Perhaps that was, and still is, the foundation of God's plans. In terms of your second question, perhaps in the tree of knowledge are the pieces needed for you to truly understand God's new plan."

"Boss, I would like to imagine that perhaps the twenty-two words I saw on the cross in my first dream have led me to think that the tree of knowledge is a very important symbol in the Bible. For years, with the help of a dictionary, I analyzed these words one at a time. As a result, I gained new knowledge and I began to see you guys in different ways."

"You sure did. Let's talk about that."

"Wow! How can I do that? Twenty-two words I have in front of me. Where should I begin, Boss?"

"Perhaps you should start from the top and work your way down. Let's see where all this will lead you. Think of all those words as pieces of a puzzle—when you find the last piece, you will have completed your vision of God's new plans."

"Okay, I'm ready to talk with you about some of these words. The first word is *control* and the last word is *simplicity*."

"Okay, now tell me in a simple way what control means to you."

"I imagine that control is one of the strong foundations we humans must have in order to not do stupid things. When we lose control, we hurt ourselves and often hurt others, especially our loved ones. Myself? I have developed a good, strong control of my inner feelings. Once in a while, I will lose control, but this only lasts for a short time. Unfortunately, many humans are suffering because other humans have used control for building up their own egos. Many millions of humans around the globe are dying of starvation or getting killed because of wars caused by control issues. Just think, we are in the twenty-first century, and we see young human beings blowing themselves up with dynamite in the name of their God, taking innocent lives along with them. I have never been able to understand the kind of power some leaders use to brainwash young adults in the name of religion or some other ideology.

"But people, especially the young, do need to learn control so as not to abuse food, drugs, alcohol, or tobacco. In my lifetime, I have read much about this matter, and I have come to the conclusion that control is what we all need. We could lay the blame on those who manufacture these products and create the television ads that brainwash the minds of young people into believing it's okay to use drugs, get drunk, or eat compulsively in order to solve their problems. But my suggestion, instead, as a father and grandfather, would be for parents to openly discuss with their young children the importance of postponing until they are at least twenty-one the use of drugs or alcohol. It is a fact that a young person's brain is not fully developed, and they are not strong enough to have adequate control over their actions. In many cases, suicide seems to offer young persons addicted to drugs or alcohol the only way out of their misery. In a nutshell, I would say to young people, you have lots of time left to get high or to get drunk. In reality, every human has some bad moments in life. That's when control comes in handy. When you have control, you will have a better life, not only for yourself, but also for those who love you."

"Good work, Joseph. Simple and to the point. What is the next word?"

"The next words are *imagination* and *knowledge*."

"Imagination? That's one of my favorite subjects. Tell me, Joseph, what imagination and knowledge mean to you."

"Imagination? It is an extraordinary word. It reminds me of the phrase by Albert Einstein that I saw in my first dream: 'Imagination is more important than knowledge.' I think that phrase was the beginning of a new me. Since then, every day, I have explored new imaginary visions that have been very clear in my mind. It is as if I was gaining a new awareness—the ability to imagine the future by accepting the power of imagination."

"Well put, my dear friend."

"Boss, this is the first time you have called me a 'dear friend.' Thanks."

"Didn't we make an agreement at the beginning that we would also be good friends?"

"Of course, Boss. I just felt very overwhelmed when you called me your dear friend. You see, Boss, friendship means a lot to me. In my life, I have had two very good friends. One was Tanino. Tanino and I shared everything imaginable. We were best friends from the time we were very young until his death a few years ago. If it is possible, I would like to imagine that Tanino, wherever he is, could somehow also be a part of God's new plan for the afterlife. He was a very good person and loved by everyone. I highly recommend him. You know what I mean, my dear friend?"

"I knew that. One day you will see Tanino's participation."

"Thanks, Boss. The other dear friend is Joe, another Joe, Joe Tobia, a university professor with a vast store of knowledge. He is a great person and a great friend. Since the day I first met him over thirty years ago, we have gotten along well together. For hours I could freely share with him everything about my dreams, visions, and life. He is a good listener and very knowledgeable and always gave me good advice. His teaching was very unique, simple, and right to the point. To me, a best friend and a good teacher is one who never judges you and who supports you unconditionally. Anyway, back to the world of the imagination. I strongly believe that imagination is the road that leads to new awareness."

"Good work, Joseph. What is the next word?"

"The next word is *family*."

"That's another important word. Tell me what family

means to you."

"Family means a lot to me. I was blessed with great parents. They were simple people who dedicated their lives to keeping the family together. They always made sure that my sisters and I had a place to live and plenty of food to eat. They gave me unconditional love and respect and taught me to always respect others if you want respect in return. The foundation my parents gave me has been very good for my self-esteem. I have tried to share these qualities with my three beautiful children and two special grandchildren. In order to have a good family, we all must give unconditional love and respect. That is what family means to me."

"Bravo, Giuseppe, right to the roots. You don't mind if I also call you Giuseppe?"

"Of course you can. I have used several different names throughout my life, and I have asked myself why."

"By using different names, you gain different personalities. This makes your inner life easier, as you can accept all those visions your mind has encountered."

"I see what you mean, Boss. By giving each a name, I was able to give each one a personality, plus a vision along with a task. I guess that's where imagination takes over, isn't it?"

"It sure is. Like Albert Einstein said, 'Imagination is more important than knowledge,' and what you always say is, 'With imagination, anything is possible.' What is the next word?"

"The next word is *home*."

"Home—a very interesting concept. What is your definition of home?"

"Let me see, Boss. How can I tell you how important it is to have a comfortable home, especially when you are older and have children. I don't understand how we have so many homeless people—especially young people—living on the streets. That's not right, Boss. Humans have made so many wonderful discoveries, but they are not smart enough to build homes for the many millions who do not have them. Boss, do you think humans one day will solve this problem?"

"They may one day, but you must first find a way for those who have the know-how to start to soften their human conscience and human ego. You know what I am talking about, don't you?"

"Sure I do. That is Don Quixote's mission, and now it is mine, too."

"What is the next word?"

"The next word is *responsibility*."

"Another important word. Share with me how responsibility has affected your life."

"Responsibility to me begins at a very young age. For example, a child should listen to his parents about taking daily responsibility inside the house. Other examples of taking responsibility are getting to school on time and paying attention to the teachers. Then when you start to work, it is very important always to be on time. If you aren't on time, eventually you may get fired.

"In my case, I took responsibility very seriously and always had a good attitude toward my daily work activities. I never lost a job because I always did my work as best as I could. The same goes for family life. It is also true that it is very important to have the proper education or a good trade to make a decent living. My father always told me that nobody gives you anything for nothing. You must earn it. Do you get my point?"

"Of course I do, but I see that many humans never learn to take their responsibilities seriously, and consequently, many of their lives are very sad and empty. That's not right. What is the next word?"

"The next word concerns *work*."

"Work. That fits in with what you have said about responsibility. Tell me, Pippo, about work."

"It's funny that you now call me Pippo, like when I was a boy. I started to work when I was about eight years old, and I always took my work very seriously and tried to do my best. In my lifetime, I have learned several trades using my hands: I have been a tailor, a barber, a hairdresser, and a cook. My first paid job was as a hairdresser when I was eighteen after I emigrated to Venezuela. About six months into it, I started earning a good salary. Then, after I emigrated to America, I spent my first twenty years working as a hairdresser in New York City. I always made a very good living. Along the way, I had my own beauty salon. The same was true when I began to work as a cook—I had five pizzerias and made a very good living. I always took a lot of pride in my work. For me, work was enjoyment, not just a job. And whatever I was doing, I always did my best to improve. I guess my message to young people is that we all must work if we want to take care of ourselves. It is in our DNA. Believe me, it will enrich one's whole life. It is much better when you can give as well as receive. That's what work means to me."

"Pippo, I like the way you have explained that. What is the next word?"

"The next word is *motivation*."

"Motivation, another important word. Enrico, tell me what motivation means to you."

"You know, Boss, I knew that with this word, you would call me Enrico—this was the nickname I was given at my first job in America, because there already was a Giuseppe at the hair salon. To me, motivation is the internal structure we use to make ourselves successful in whatever we are doing. In my case, I remember when I lived in New York City and I was working as a hairdresser, I was overwhelmed when I watched and met many successful people. I observed how they were dressed and how they behaved, and those experiences showed me how important it was for me to motivate myself if I wanted to be successful and a part of that world. For most of my working years, especially as a boss myself, I applied these ideas of motivation not only to myself, but to my employees as well. Their work performance improved, and as a consequence, they were able to earn good salaries and were very proud of themselves. In my life, I have loved motivating people, especially young people. Enrico was a very talented character and was very good at teaching his way. That's what motivation means to me."

"I know that. I was there watching you, too. You and Enrico should always be very proud of how you motivated yourself, as well as others."

"Boss, I think that was one chapter in my life that I will never forget. Lots of work and lots of fun. Anyway, the next word is *security*."

"Giuseppe, what does security mean to you?"

"Perhaps the need for security is the leading cause for a person's building a very strong foundation. In my experience, I believe that when you have mastered how to make money, you consequently gain security and are able to meet your basic needs for survival. Then you can focus better on achieving your goals, whatever they may be. In my case, I am now retired, and my pension is my security. I now have the time and the freedom to write about my dreams and visions. I have a wonderful wife and a beautiful family. That's my security."

"Well put—simple and direct. Bravo, Giuseppe! And, by the way, congratulations on your recent marriage. What is the next word?"

"Thanks, Boss. The next word is *foundation*."

"Foundation. It's getting better. Enrico, tell me what foundation means to you."

"It is a little complicated to talk about foundation. In order to accomplish a project, we need to build a strong foundation to promote it successfully. If we want to have a mate and live together happily, we must build a strong foundation of the things that make us content. With the good and the bad in a relationship, we have to learn to compromise so that the relationship works. The same goes for making a strong family foundation. Then there is another important foundation—one that has to do with what God has created on Earth for us humans, such as the trees and flowers that show their beauty every year. That's what foundation means to me.

"My next word is *success*, but Boss, I need a rest. I want to share with you my present state of mind."

"Whatever it is, I am a good listener. What's on your mind?"

"The way my life is going, it won't be too long before I will be going public with the concept of God's plan for the afterlife. You see, Boss, for some reason, it is important for me to have the moral support of my family if or when that should happen."

"I am sure they will support you in whatever way you need."

"I hope so. Their support will be my foundation to continue believing without any reservations."

"Stay warm, Joe. I will talk with you later."

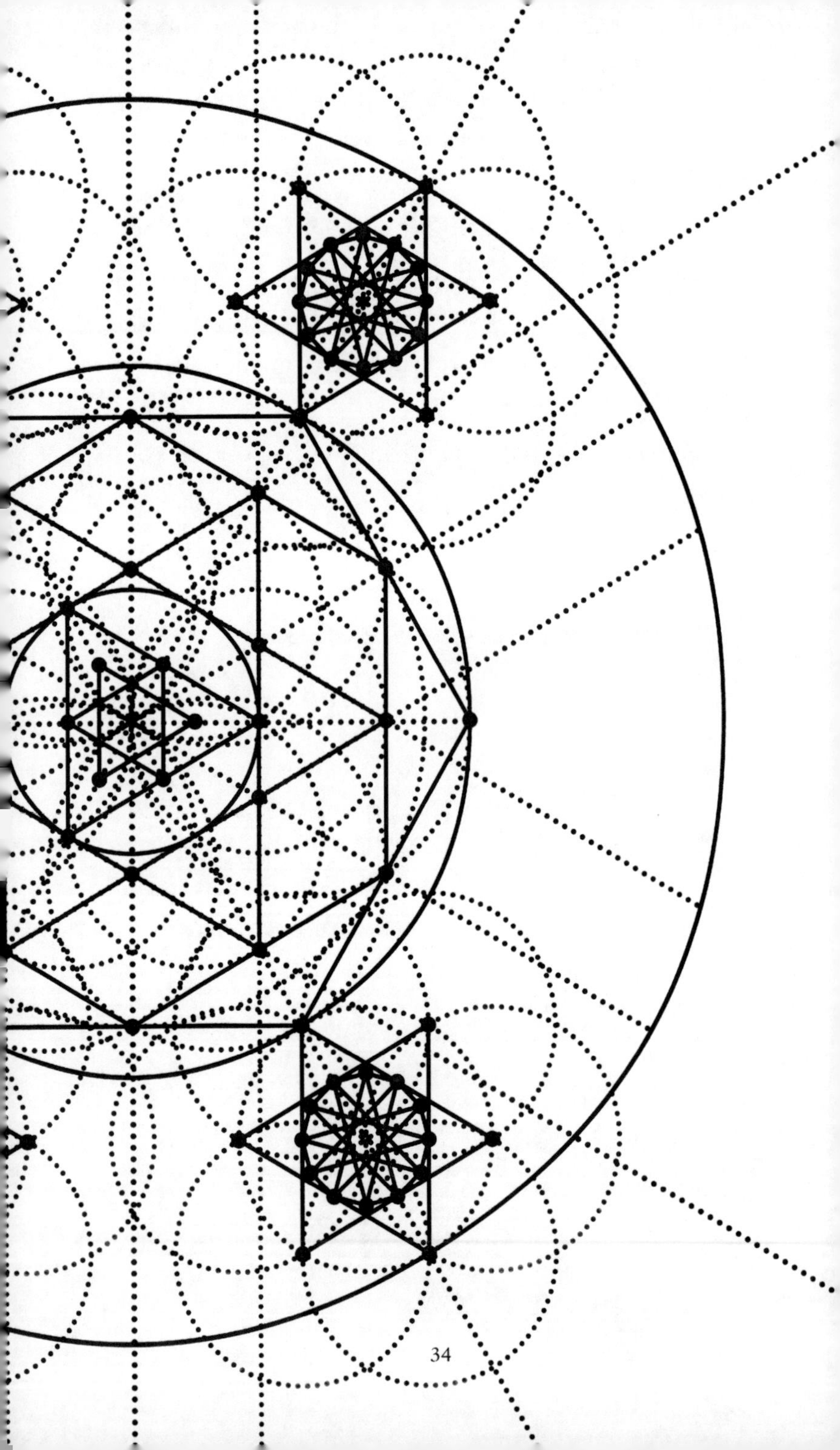

CHAPTER 5

*Conversation with My Granddaughter: A Vision of the Afterlife*

One day when I was visiting my fourteen-year-old granddaughter, Katrina, I was telling her about my dream for constructing a new world for the afterlife. She was excited about my story and asked me many questions about what this world would be like.

"Nonno, why and how would this new world be constructed?"

"Good question, Katrina. I will try to answer the best way I can. Since the beginning of God's creation, there has been much written about the eternal life that Jesus spoke of, and there have been many visions given of what it might be like. In my dreams, Michelangelo has designed a blueprint for the world of the afterlife, but first, with the help of technology, science must create a quantum computer like Albert Einstein had envisioned. That will be a bridge for communication with the souls. When that is accomplished, we will begin the structure of a new world for all the souls. My understanding is that this new world will be constructed first as a model inside the sea."

"Inside the sea?" asked Katrina.

"Yes! You heard right. Inside the sea."

"But how can that be done?"

"Well, let me try to explain this vision to you. It all began with an incredible dream I had about forty years ago, in 1977. In that dream, I was chosen by seven souls once well known on Earth—Albert Einstein, Pope John XXIII, Orson Wells, Sigmund Freud, Nostradamus, Khalil Gibran, and Michelangelo. They were known as the Spiritual Commission of the Souls and lived on the invisible planet of Iyakacquasia, and they asked me to be their intermediary for sharing with scientists this new concept of what the afterlife could be. In the beginning, it was very difficult to understand what they were saying, but along the way, I had in my dreams many dialogues with each of these souls, which made their mission clearer to me."

"What kind of dialogues did you have with these people?"

"It went something like this: I said to Albert Einstein, 'After many years of research, I am convinced that we are on the right track for building a quantum computer capable of being a bridge of communication with the souls. Currently, scientists scattered in many parts of the globe have much of the knowledge necessary to build such a computer. Still, as far as I know, no one talks about your vision. And if there are scientists who imagine this vision, perhaps fear takes over—the fear of being taken as a fool.'

"In another dream, I had a conversation with Nostradamus. As I looked into the future to see what I was supposed to do, it seemed to be a very complex undertaking. But after talking with Nostradamus, I better understood. He put in my mind the power to see the future.

"Then I spoke with Sigmund Freud. The conversation with him led me to understand that dreaming is a big part of life—much has been written on this subject. Now I see that a dream left uninterpreted is like having a book that has never been opened. I understand that dreams have the power to reveal a new awareness.

"Then, when I spoke with Michelangelo, I said to him, 'Now I am at your command. Use my hands so that with the help of technology, I will be able to visually transform the blueprint that you have put into my mind.' And then my dialogues were finished."

"Could you tell me more about your dream about creating a world of the afterlife inside the sea? That sounds weird. I can't understand how that would work."

"I'll try my best to explain it to you. It's difficult even for me to understand. With the help of a human's DNA, each soul would be a clone that would appear similar to how the person appeared on Earth. For example, they would look somewhat like the animated characters you see in the movies or on TV."

"But how can these clones live inside the sea? How do they breathe? And wouldn't they always be bumping into fish—or, heavens, even get killed by a shark?"

"The clones will have a protective shield around them and will be able to breathe as they did on Earth. Don't worry about the fish. They will swim around them."

"Okay, that answers my question even though I still don't understand why this afterlife is going to be inside the sea."

"My understanding is that this is a trial model of an afterlife that will eventually be moved to a far-off planet. But for now, the sea offers the large area that is needed for developing this world without interfering with any country's land."

"That sounds interesting, but I'm wondering what everyday life would be like in the sea?"

"It will be similar to the setup on Earth. For example, there will be housing, streets, fields, restaurants, schools, theaters, cars, and so on. And that, I imagine, is one of the reasons God needs our help to build this kind of afterlife. Perhaps, for those who will obtain eternal life."

"Another question. What about money there?"

"In that world, there will be no money, so there will be no cause for greed and wars."

"No money? How can people have houses and everything without money? That doesn't make sense."

"People will use their knowledge to make or do whatever they are capable of. In exchange, they will receive what they need for living a pleasant life. All occupations will be treated with respect, so that, for example, the farmer, worker, or the waiter will receive the same compensation as the owner of a business or a professor."

"Oh, I like that everyone is respected for their work. I have another question on a different topic. You know how I like to play soccer? Will there be sports there, and what about competing? That doesn't seem to fit in a place for the afterlife."

"There will be only friendly competition. There will be sports, but in the games, the competition will be to challenge the players to do their best while at the same time providing them satisfaction and physical exercise. The same will go for actors and musicians. The main purpose will be for them to perform at their best, not only for themselves, but also for the good of the community. Their rewards come from knowing that they have developed their capabilities to the best of their ability, and that they have brought pleasure to those in the audience."

"That makes a lot of sense. I know that I feel good when I've tried my best in a game or at school. That's more important than winning to me. I have even more questions. How does the clone eat and travel? Where do they live? What are their houses like?"

"Wow! You do have a lot of questions. I'll try my best, but I still don't have all of the details of how this life will be. As you know, the sea is rich in foods that humans on Earth are able to eat. So it will be with the clones—this food will provide the nutrition they need. However, they will mainly eat in order to maintain their energy—there will not be the same pleasure connected with eating certain foods that we on Earth have. Their feelings in this way are a little different."

"Oh, that seems a bit sad to me for them not to enjoy something like ice cream or pizza."

"Let me try to be a little clearer. They will be able to make these foods we have on Earth, but like I said, their relationship to food is a bit different than ours."

"Now what about travel? Do they just swim around in the ocean to get where they want to go? That could get tiring."

"They can swim, but to travel longer distances, they will have a propeller attached to their backs."

"That sounds like a lot of fun! And what kind of houses will they have?"

"First of all, in order to be able to use certain materials for housing, there will be large areas protected by invisible shields to build the houses in. They will be of different sizes and designs according to what each clone wants. Later, I'll show you some pictures of the kinds of structures Michelangelo has in mind from his blueprint."

"Nonno, what kinds of jobs will there be in the afterlife? Will they be different from here? Oh, I just had an interesting thought. Will there be a need for doctors and social workers if the afterlife is a utopia?"

"Those are great questions! My understanding is that they will continue with the work they did on Earth if they found pleasure in this work. They will have the opportunity to gain even greater skills and knowledge than they had before. For those who had jobs they did not like, they will be able to explore other fields of work, and then they will choose an occupation that will bring them satisfaction."

"And what about doctors and social workers?"

"There will still be a need for these occupations, but their work will be different. Social workers will be busy helping those who want to choose a new occupation. They will have the skills to guide them in finding the correct job. Doctors now will be freed from treating diseases, and they will be doing research to improve the clones' lives and the environment in which they live."

"If there is no money and they don't get paid but have all the necessities of life, why should they even work?"

"You have to understand that even though this is a utopia, everyone still has to have responsibilities and motivation like on Earth."

"What do you mean by that? I would think that especially those who had worked hard on Earth would just like to rest all the time."

"How would you feel spending every day at home doing nothing but resting and watching television?"

"Oh, that would soon get very boring."

"That's exactly my point. Even in the afterlife, there are rules to be followed, and one of the rules is that everyone contributes to the society by working."

"What if someone wants to get something like a car or a computer—how does he or she get it if there's no money?"

"It would work like a bartering system. Do you remember when I told you about how my father got paid for making shoes or cutting hair? His customers would pay him back with cheese, flour, or other things in exchange for his work. That is how the clones will get what they want. It sounds a bit complicated, but a good system of bartering will be established that will work for all the clones."

"Who makes the rules and figures out how the bartering system works?"

"All I know is that people who were skilled in detail

work on Earth will be handling these kinds of questions. By the way, Katrina, I like your questions even though some of them are too difficult for me to answer right now."

"Here's a good question, Nonno. When people die, will they keep their same age in eternal life?"

"That's a difficult question to answer. I really don't know. If someone dies at the age of ninety, will that person still be ninety in the eternal life? Perhaps in the eternal life, there is no illness or disease, so older people will be able to enjoy only the benefits of age like giving wise counsel to younger people."

"What about children that live in this afterlife? Are babies born there, or are the children there those who died on Earth?"

"I think the children would be those who had been killed or died on Earth. They would become a part of a family, especially for those couples who were never able to have children on Earth but wanted them."

"Wow! There are a lot of difficult questions to think about. I'm also curious if there will be a common language, or does each clone speak the language he or she spoke on Earth? If there are multiple languages, do the clones understand each other?"

"I am not sure, but I would imagine that with the benefit of technology, everyone would be able to understand all languages."

"That would be neat. Then kids there wouldn't have to take French, Spanish, or especially German or Chinese. Speaking of learning new things, would it be possible to learn how to play an instrument, or to paint, or so on? Are there teachers for learning these new things?"

"One of the big joys of eternal life that I imagine is that people will have the time to learn things that they did not have the opportunity to learn on Earth. For instance, if in your life on Earth you had the dream of becoming an actor, a musician, or an artist, now you would be able to fulfill this dream. So you see, many teachers will have work to do in the eternal life."

"What an imagination! What a beautiful picture of the afterlife! Now here's a question that I think a lot of people wonder about. How are the relationships with people they once knew on Earth? For example, if someone was married several times, who will be their partner in the afterlife?"

"As Jesus said in the Bible when answering a similar question, there is no marriage in heaven. So I'm not sure about what the exact nature of these relationships would be. However, I would imagine that relationships between people would be amicable. I would hope that those relationships that on Earth had been bad and had been broken would be healed in the afterlife."

"Along those same lines, do the clones have feelings

like we do here on Earth? Do they become attached to others as they did on Earth?"

"I would imagine that their feelings would be more like a robot's feelings."

"That's strange. What do you mean by that?"

"Well, let me try to explain. For example, when clones eat delicious ice-cream cones, the pleasure they would experience would come from an electronic impulse that would give them the feeling similar to what we feel when we get goose pimples. Above all, the electronic feelings would prevent them from experiencing the strong, destructive feelings of anger, hate, and sadness. Underlying their emotional life would be a feeling of calm and peacefulness."

"Okay, one last question. What about the clones' connection to God, Jesus, and the Holy Spirit? Will they finally get to see them face-to-face?"

"Oh, I am sorry to disappoint you, but the clones still have more work to do before that happens. Albert Einstein once said something like this: 'We must explore new worlds before we meet God face-to-face.' I take this to mean that the clones now liberated from many of the struggles on Earth will have time to communicate more deeply with God. Then, eventually, they will see God face-to-face."

"I have loved asking you all these questions and

hearing your answers. Your vision of the afterlife is beautiful. You're right. With imagination, everything is possible."

"Thank you so much, sweetheart, for your questions and for letting me share with you my vision of the afterlife."

The End (*or maybe, The Beginning...*)

# ACKNOWLEDGMENTS

I would like to give special thanks to Nancy Torgove Clasby. Reading her book, *The Reluctant Mystic*, helped me find the courage to publish my story. It told me I wasn't the only one who'd had this kind of awakening. She also helped me better understand my own mystical experience. I hope that one day I will have the pleasure of meeting Nancy in person.

A special thanks to my wonderful wife, Judy, for never giving up on me. She is my angel. In my heart, she will always be my angel. Judy, I love you.

My special thanks, as well, to you, the reader. I hope that after reading my story, you will come to a deeper understanding of the nature of God and God's plan for the afterlife.

*Little Giuseppe with his sisters Tanina and Giovanna (left and right) and mother, Grazia, 1946.*

*Father, Vito, as a child musician, circa 1920.*

*Giuseppe as a hairdresser in Venezuela, 1958.*

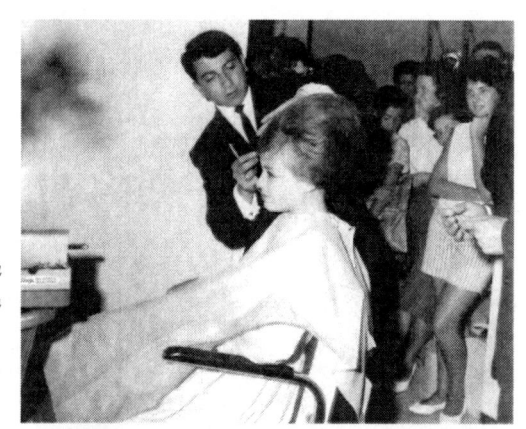

*Giuseppe as a hairdresser in Hartford, Connecticut, 1960.*

*Giuseppe (center), owner of a New York City beauty salon, with his stylists, 1973.*

*Tanino, Giuseppe, and Gigi, teenage friends in Sicily, 1956.*

**GIUSEPPE GIUCASTRO** was born in Buccheri, Sicily. He immigrated to the United States in 1960, where he lived the American dream, first gaining success as a hairdresser in New York City and, later, as the owner of a pizzeria in Connecticut. In his thirties, Giucastro experienced a different kind of dream, one that inspired him to write. This is his first book, and he hopes there will be many more to come.